D1199044

THE ART OF STENCIL

THE ART OF STENCIL

History and Modern Uses

Norman Laliberté   Alex Mogelon

An Art Horizons Book

Van Nostrand Reinhold Company
New York Cincinnati London Toronto Melbourne

To Jesse

Design Consultant: Milton Glaser
Type set by Lettick Typografic, Inc.
Printed by Halliday Lithograph Corporation
Bound by Complete Books Company
Color printed by Toppan Printing Co., Ltd.

Published by Van Nostrand Reinhold Company
A Division of Litton Educational Publishing, Inc.
450 West 33rd Street, New York, N.Y. 10001
Published simultaneously in Canada by
Van Nostrand Reinhold Ltd.

16 15 14 13 12 11 10 9 8 7 6 5 4 3 2 1

Also by the authors:
Twentieth Century Woodcuts (1971)
Collage, Montage, Assemblage (1971)
Drawing with Ink (1970)
Drawing with Pencils (1969)
Silhouettes, Shadows and Cutouts (1968)
Painting with Crayons (1967)
Banners and Hangings by Norman Laliberté
and Sterling McIlhany (1966)
Wooden Images by Norman Laliberté
and Maureen Jones (1966)

Opposite Page

A stencil decoration
typical of the Victorian
era. Simple stencil
patterns were immensely
popular during this period
for decorating ceilings
and hallways and as
ornamental borders.
(Reproduced courtesy
Dover Publications, Inc.)

Frontispiece:
No. 39. Oil crayon
drawing by
Norman Laliberté.

Contents

1.
Early Uses of the Stencil

The stencil is one of the earliest decorative forms known to man. It was used by the Egyptians of the pyramid era, by the Chinese at the time they built the Great Wall, and by both primitive and civilized people throughout the world in almost every historic age which required decorative patterns and images on a repeat or multiple basis.

The basic stencil process has remained the same throughout the ages. An open image, design or pattern is drawn onto and then cut out of an impervious piece of material. The material (which is now a stencil) is pressed or held flat against the object to be decorated, and color in the form of paint, crayon (or whatever medium is being used) is applied by brushing, dabbing or filling in the open or cut-out areas of the stencil. This open stencil method was common to early civilizations in decorating interior and exterior walls, furnishings, fabrics, wares, and utensils.

Stencilling has been a decorative technique of primitive peoples in many places, including the South Pacific and North and Central America, and is believed to have predated by many centuries the European influence in these areas. Applications of stencil designs are evident on many pieces of American Indian ceramics dating back to prehistoric times. The first explorers of the Fiji Islands were surprised to see beautiful geometric designs printed onto coarse bark cloth by means of stencils cut out of banana leaves.

There are many early evidences of the use of stencils among so-called civilized people. It is known that the stencil was used by early Greek and Etruscan civilizations and that Buddhist artists of several thousand years ago decorated early temples and monasteries by means of stencil art.

There are many instances of the use of stencil in producing religious manuscripts dating from the period 600-800 A.D. At that time it was used not only as a means of producing a repetitive, decorative element but of duplicating words as well as a primitive form of printing. Authentic examples of Japanese cloth decorated with designs applied by the stencil process go back to the year 710 A.D. The stencil has been an integral element in Japanese folk art and textile printing throughout the known history of that nation.

The introduction of paper into Europe brought with it many opportunities for stencilling, which already was popular as a decorative art in many countries on that continent prior to the Middle Ages. Embroidery and tapestry, carving in wood, glass, precious metals, and ivory — produced by means of the stencil process — were quite common in cathedrals and wealthy manors of the time. Many people of lesser means used the stencil also to apply decorative touches to and beautify walls, floors, and furniture.

There is a close alliance between the early European use of stencils and the development of printing with wood blocks and then with movable type. The earliest playing cards we know — dating from the year 1440 — are believed by some to have been produced by means of stencil. The playing cards which followed — and to an extent manuscripts, decorative sheets, and religious renderings — were printed by woodcut and wood block, then hand-colored by stencil application of paint or ink. Printing and stencil decorating (or "enlivening," as it was sometimes called) worked hand in hand in this manner in many instances from the 15th to 19th century.

In the 17th century the stencil played a major part in the development of the wallpaper industry. Pioneered by Jean Papillon of France, matching wallpaper sheets known as "domino" papers were colored and printed by stencil and became popular throughout Europe. The stencil also became available for decorating individual pieces of furniture, panels, and repeat borders on walls and floors. Its popularity as a decorative art form was immediately prevalent in early America and was common in homes throughout Massachusetts, Connecticut, Rhode Island, Vermont, New York, New Hampshire, Ohio, and Maine as far back as the late 1700s. The United Empire Loyalists fleeing north from this area during the American Revolution (1776-1787) brought some aspects of stencil art to their new homes in Upper and Lower Canada and the Atlantic Provinces.

It has been maintained that some of the more similar cave drawings dating back tens of thousands of years may have been produced by means of a primitive stencil or form-tracing process of one kind or another. Though the creating of a stencil itself requires the skill of an artist or craftsman, stencil application in most cases is a simple process within the range of most people's ability. This ready accessibility to almost everyone, along with the practicality of immediate result, has been responsible for the great popularity and personal charm of the stencil as a decorative art and a recreational activity for hundreds of years.

In this Victorian stencil the heaviness of the dark lines and the lightness of the curved scroll and circle forms tend to compete with each other to produce a well-balanced and pleasing design.

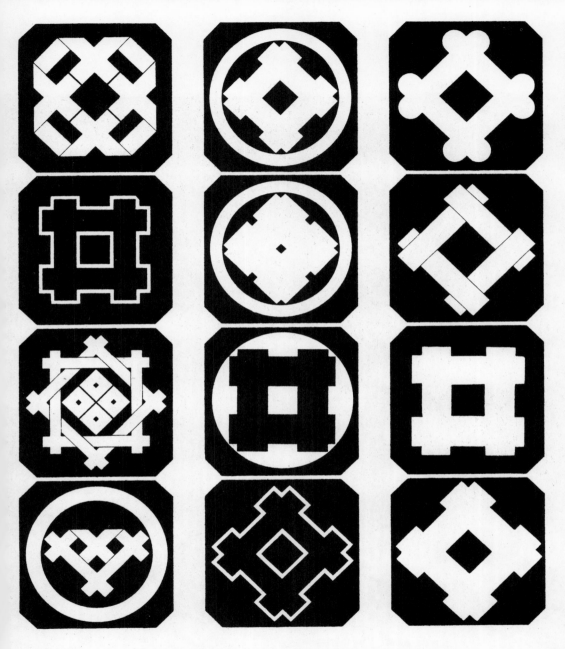

A series of Japanese family crests. These seem to be similarly shaped in tic-tac-toe style, yet each crest is entirely different from the others. Some of the designs are open, others criss-cross, still others are closed, filled in or varied with round edges or square corners. Japanese stencil designs, such as these, many times were based on religious or mythological concepts.

A Japanese stencil-letter written during the mid-nineteenth century. Though these letter forms are old, their flow and placement have something of a contemporary sophistication about them.

This Japanese stencil designed for fabric printing goes in a vertical and horizontal direction simultaneously. The interplay of fine against heavy lines gives the composition a feeling of kinetic energy. Designs such as this were cut into stiff paper with knives and punches and were used to print cotton and silk fabrics. (Reproduced courtesy Dover Publications, Inc.)

Examples of the Polish folk art known as *wycinanki*. The symbols and designs (inspired by folklore and religion) are cut out of paper with coarse shears and can be used decoratively as stencils. The rural inhabitants of Poland have been creating intricate designs like these since the 18th century.

Detail of a vase made *circa* 1200 B.C. depicting Mycenaean warriors marching to battle. Note the stencilled decorative border in both the background and foreground. The decorative elements on many Greek vases of this era were combinations of drawing and stencil detail. (Reproduced courtesy National Museum, Athens.)

Opposite Page

Primitive pottery designs from Santo Domingo, Nicaragua. The basically simple forms are intermingled, reversed, painted in varying colors, and positioned so as to create still other designs and an effective result. Many primitive decorative themes in practically all parts of the world are perpetuated by means of the stencil process.

An Indian blanket of
mountain-goat wool from
Tlingit, Alaska. The
design is totem-like; each
individual element within
the composition has its
own meaning, though
there is no exact
interpretation of the story
portrayed by the overall
blanket.

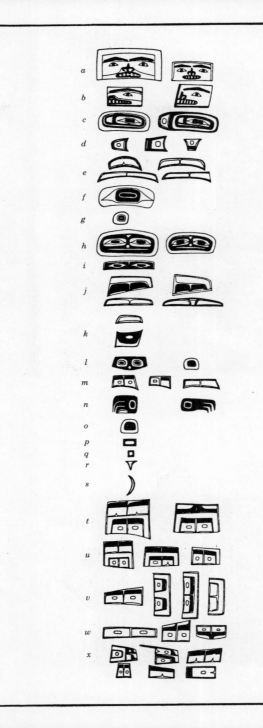

The individual design elements frequently were perpetuated from one generation to another and executed in stencil form. Images illustrated include: (a) full face; (b) profile; (c) salmon trout head; (d) filler; (e) eyebrow; (f) joint; (g), (l), (o) interchangeable as black eye; (h), (i) goggle; (j) mouth design; (k) cheek; (1) nostril; (m) wing design; (n) hand; (p), (q) side holes or rain drops; (r) woman's hair ornament; (s) slit; (t), (u), (v), (w), (x) winged feathers.

17

Above. 15th century Florentine wall panels on which the backgrounds are stencilled in the imitation of a textile. (Reproduced courtesy of the Staats Museum, Berlin.)

Below, left. Coptic design of the 4th century. (Reproduced courtesy of the Cairo Museum.)

Below, right. Mohammedan motif of 8th-century Persia. (Reproduced courtesy of the Louvre, Paris.) Through the stencil technique, themes such as these appeared in the wall and floor designs of many public places.

Opposite Page

A painting of the late 17th century from the Northern Dvina River area of Russia. The composition which depicts a popular folk tale, has stencilled decorative images and details; it was painted on the side of a wooden chest.

18

A page from a stencilled hymnal made in 1755. This Book of the Mass was stencilled in red and black ink for the Augustinian Monastery at **Laos, Flanders (Belgium)**, by U. Boddaert. (Reproduced courtesy of the Library of the School of Music at Yale University.)

Opposite Page

Left. An array of metal stencils designed by Moses Eaton of Hancock, New Hampshire, used early in the 19th century to decorate walls.

Right. Wall decorations in the Manuel Alcock House, Hancock, New Hampshire. Stencilled designs such as these on walls, floors, and furniture were an important decorative art in pioneer America, particularly in the New England states. (Reproduced courtesy Dover Publications, Inc.)

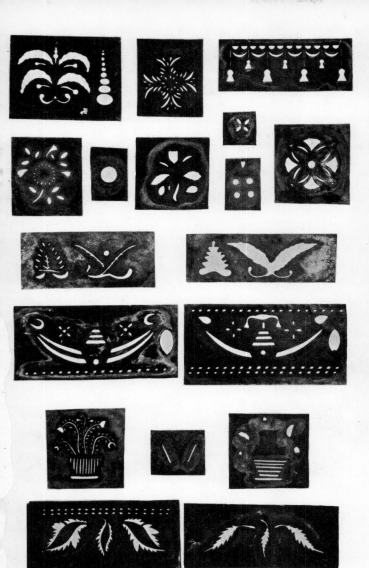

A Mexican folk art rendering with very intricate design elements in the form of a skeletal procession. The entire composition has been cut out of soft tissue paper by a stencil-like device much in the manner of a paper doily. Compositions such as this vary in size from large proportions to intricate miniatures. This example is two feet in width.

23

Opposite Page

Patriotic stencil designs
from a children's activity
book produced by the
Stencil Art Publishing
Co., Bedford, Ohio.

Another stencil from the
same book. Designs such
as these were used as
school projects and for
the making of posters.

25

DURO DECAL CO. INC.

1832 JUNEWAY TERRACE CHICAGO, 26 ILL.

DURO

A B C D E F G !

H I J K L M N :

O P Q R S T U ;

V W X Y Z & $

1 2 3 4 5 6 7 8 9

DURO LETTERING GUIDE NO. 22 ROMAN 1"

PUNCH OUT ALL LETTERS, FIGURES & INDICATOR HOLES

SEE ENVELOPE FOR DIRECTIONS, FOR SIZES & STYLES AVAILABLE

2.
The Stencil in Industry and Advertising

Screen-printing of fabrics is perhaps one of the principal industries spawned by the advent of the stencil. The Japanese originated and perfected fabric-printing stencils in the late 17th century, drawing on their rich heritage of folklore, legend, and religious mysticism for subject matter. Images of geese, waves, chrysanthemums, leaves, crayfish, grapes, flower baskets, tigers, fir cones, peacock feathers, ducks, and other animals and objects have become classics in Japanese art, perpetuated by stencil repetition.

The screen or stencil technique for printing fabrics on a mass basis originated in Germany in the mid-1800s and was brought to Japan late in that century and to the United States by 1905. By 1915 the photographic screen for fabric printing was patented as were a number of multicolor fabric-printing processes, and by 1925 apparatus for the screen stencilling of full bolts of silk and cotton was being developed. Processes for fabric printing are continually being improved and expanded and today include the manufacture and printing of materials that have popularized the "fake" or "fun" fur industries.

Communication has also been a vital function of the stencil in addition to its many-faceted attributes in the decorative arts. Individual stencil letters or alphabet forms may well have originated at the time when manuscripts were being mass-decorated through this medium. Stencil signing and stencil addressing were extremely popular in pioneering America because of ready availability, ease of application, and clarity of finished product. Today, stencils are used when quick and inexpensive signs are required and in instances when particular qualities or conditions such as "fragile," "danger" or "breakable" require emphasis.

In our age of sophisticated letter styles, the almost bare detail qualities of stencil lettering attract immediate attention and observation. Designers seeking new and different approaches to graphics for book and record jackets, posters, billboard and advertising layouts have discovered that stencil-styled lettering in its proper environment has unique and individual characteristics capable of enhancing the communicative aspects of their work. Attracted by the unique qualities of the stencil line, graphic artists have developed a number of distinguished contemporary stencil type faces.

One of the most futuristic letter or alphabet faces we have today is the type used by computers. The computer alphabet is surprisingly stencil-like in character because its structure is solid and could well serve as a contemporary stencil form.

In fact, the computer itself is one of the most sophisticated stencil devices that man has ever developed. It, too, works on the cutout principle, for when the prearranged holes punched in the card or tape match or connect with an electronic impulse, a device is activated to automatically produce the information required. It is a far cry from primitive geometric designs being cut into broad banana leaves for the purpose of decorating a piece of raw cloth. But, somehow, the basic principles involved in both processes are startling, for they are identical in concept and approach to basic human negative and positive values.

Above. An everyday celluloid stencil used by chemistry students to illustrate their experiments.

Below. "The British Are Coming!" An advertisement for an Exhibition of Designers and Art Directors of London sponsored by the Jeffries Banknote Company, Los Angeles. A stencil is used to mark the destination of the shipment; the sender has provided further embellishment by painting a British flag within the structure of the crate.

MNBMHG MNFRT@A2BVCMNB,MJLDIOLM..,.,L IH....MMBJR M,,MM

```
0000000000000 0 0 0000 0000000000 0 000000000000000000 00000000000000000000000000000000000
1 2 3 4 5 6 7 8 9 10 11 12 13 14 15 16 17 18 19 20 21 22 23 24 25 26 27 28 29 30 31 32 33 34 35 36 37 38 39 40 41 42 43 44 45 46 47 48 49 50 51 52 53 54 55 56 57 58 59 60 61 62 63 64 65 66 67 68 69 70 71 72 73 74 75 76 77 78 79 80
1111111111111 1111 11111111111111111111111111111111 11111111111111111111111111111111111111
222 22222222222 2222 2222222222222222222222222222 22222222222222222222222222222222222222222
3333333333 333333 333 33 333 3 33 333 33333333 33333333333333333333333333333333333333
44 444 4444 44444 444 444444 444444444444444 44444 44 44444444444444444444444444444444
5 555555 5555555 55 555555555555555555555555555555555555555555555555555555555555555555555
6666666666 666666666666666 6 66666666666666666666666666666666666666666666666666666666666
77777 777777777777777777777777777777777777777777777777777777777777777777777777777777777777
8888 88888888 88888888 88888888 888 88888888 8888888888888888888888888888888888888
999999999 999 9999999999 9999999999 9999999999 99999999999999999999999999999999999999999
1 2 3 4 5 6 7 8 9 10 11 12 13 14 15 16 17 18 19 20 21 22 23 24 25 26 27 28 29 30 31 32 33 34 35 36 37 38 39 40 41 42 43 44 45 46 47 48 49 50 51 52 53 54 55 56 57 58 59 60 61 62 63 64 65 66 67 68 69 70 71 72 73 74 75 76 77 78 79 80
```
IBM 5081

Above. The IBM card is a form of stencil; the arrangement of holes or apertures dictates whether or not an impulse connection is made and subsequently controls the flow of the information desired.

Below, left. A point-of-sale design by Harry Murphy for Le Fromage Gourmet Foods; note how the angle of the stencilling tends to make the lettering very dramatic.

Below, right. Examples of routing signs to the sites of various events at the 1968 Olympic Games held in Mexico designed by Peter Murdoch.

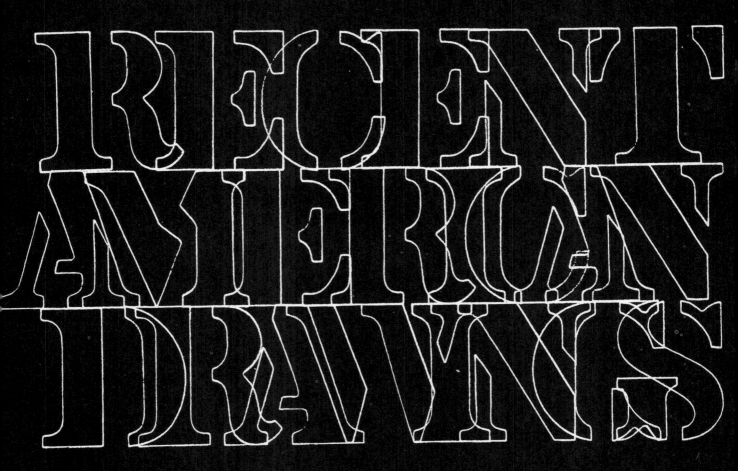

RECENT
AMERICAN
DRAWINGS

Opposite Page

A Christmas greeting in
the form of a large poster
by Jim Rapp. The word
"peace" is used in a
multitude of languages,
predominantly in stencil
type.

Cover illustration by
Carl F. Zahn for an
exhibition at the Rose Art
Museum at Brandeis
University. Though the
forms are overlapped and
compressed in space, the
eye has no trouble in
delineating individual
letters and in
distinguishing the words
almost instantly. It is a
completely different stencil
technique from that used
in the poster on page 30,
where all the letters were
filled in and stand
independently.

31

fig. 1.

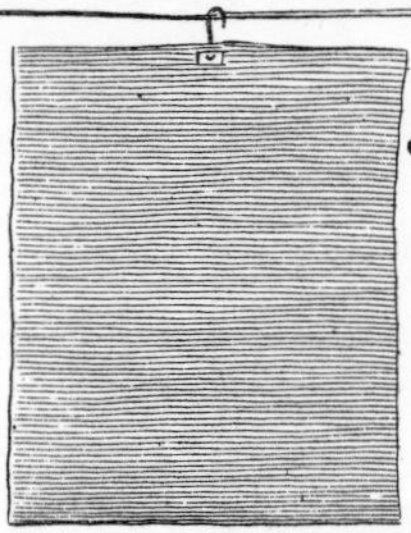

fig. 2.

fig. 6.

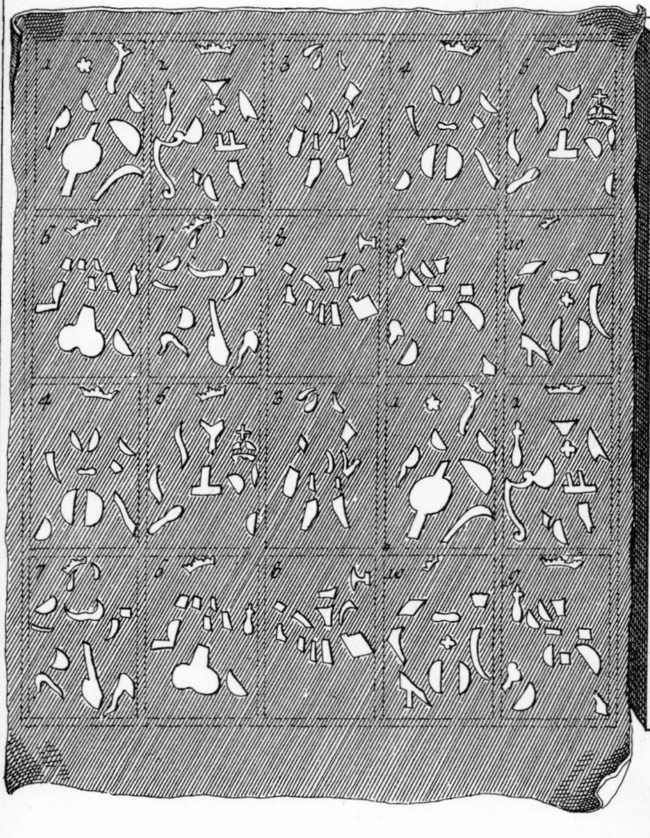

fig. 5.

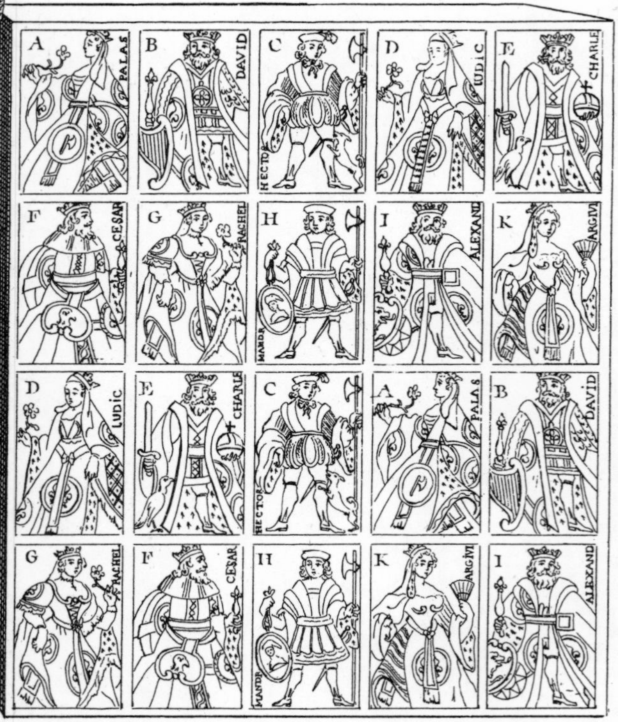

fig. 3.

fig. 4.

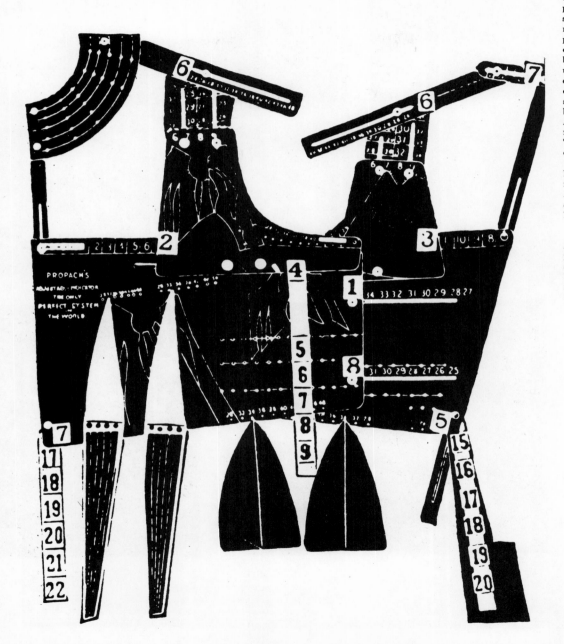

Opposite Page

The manufacture of playing cards was one of the first industrial processes in which the stencil played a major role. Here we see a block-printed sheet of playing cards with a metal stencil beside it. The stencil was used to hand-paint color elements and embellishments on the sheets (printed in black) before the cards were cut. A different stencil was required for each color. The box device is for the collating of card sets. (Reproduced courtesy of Dover Publications, Inc., from *A Diderot Pictorial Encyclopedia of Trades and Industry* by Denis Diderot.)

An old clothing pattern; patterns are a form of stencil used both in the home and throughout the industry in the manufacture of clothing.

Above. The railway is an industry in which the stencil has predominant use in both the identifying of equipment and the marking of the nature and destination of cargo. Through positioning, isolation, and the constant ravages of travel and weather which blister and distress paint, the stencilled symbol or letter takes on textures and qualities of its own and becomes an almost impressionistic painting in itself. (Reproduced courtesy of Champion Papers, a Division of U.S. Plywood Champion Papers Incorporated.)

Below, left. Cover of a folder describing a high-speed composing machine. The design by Remy Peignot projects a clever use of stencil to represent speed and motion.

Below, right. A catalog cover designed by Gerhard Doerrie for an exhibition organized by the National Gallery of Canada, Ottawa.

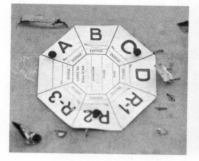

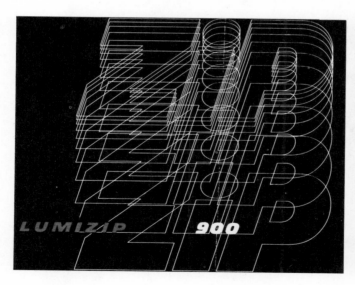
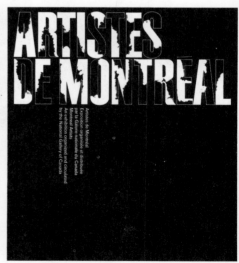

Above. No. 47 by Victor 4. Measuring 90 x 50 inches and painted on weatherproof wooden ship hatches 2 inches thick, this stencilled lettering is a comment on attendance-taking in American university classrooms. The stencil used is the same size as the width of the individual wooden planks, and this tends to cause the lines of lettering to merge and mingle with each other. The close placement of the letters at first projects a kind of overall word painting; only upon a second look does the viewer comprehend that there is a message to be deciphered. The wood is worn, and this provides texture to the letters which, though initially resembling a shipping-crate legend, somehow takes on poetic qualities.

Below, left. Markings of pavement hand-painted or sprayed through large wooden stencils.

Below, right. An old tombstone design engraved by means of a stencil.

Music Box. Wood, glass, and metal construction by Robert Rauschenberg (1951). The combination of a found crate, coarse wood, and nails which seems to match the character of the stencilled letters makes this a most interesting construction with almost medieval overtones. (Reproduced courtesy Dayton's Gallery 12, Minneapolis.)

3.
The Stencil in Contemporary Art

During the Renaissance, artists used the technique of stencil "pouncing" to transfer the outlines of preliminary drawings to walls and panel surfaces for compositions to be completed in tempera and other media. The method was simple and effective: a series of holes was punched into a large sheet of paper outlining the contour line of a drawn composition. The paper was then held against the surface of the wall or panel, and dusting powder or powdered charcoal was pounced over the holes. After the paper was removed, the dotted outline or form of the work appeared on the area to be painted. It was a convenient way of assuring proper proportions and guidelines for major paintings often being executed in difficult working areas such as ceilings and high walls.

But stencil images, forms, and letters did not appear in the compositions of fine artists until the early 1900s, when Braque and Picasso pioneered the collage medium. Commenting on this new practice, the French *avant-garde* poet and writer, Guillaume Apollinaire wrote ". . . it is perfectly legitimate to use numbers and printed letters as pictorial elements; new in art, they are already soaked with humanity." As artists experimented with pasting letters, numerals, symbols, and images onto their work, it is understandable that graphic elements applied through stencil outline tracings soon would be included as vital facets of composition expression.

There are many contemporary artists working with stencils in a wide variety of techniques; this chapter illustrates some of the variations they employ. The silk-screen work of Andy Warhol is depicted through the now familiar soup carton and the multiple-image impact of the human form and face. The stencil has been an integral ingredient in compositions by Jasper Johns, whose still-life presentations of objects and images reflect the tense complexities of the frightening technological age that is upon us. In the composition *Don't Fall and Me*, Larry Rivers not only creates forms and images by means of stencil, but includes an actual stencil as part of his collage-composition. Michael Snow uses his life-size *Walking Woman* cut-out form in an imaginative array of constructions, foldages, paintings, and collages, lending new meaning and interpretations to the environment in which the standing, flopped, folded, negative or positive figure is placed. Robert Rauschenberg creates a foreboding, medieval construction from a found crate, a fusillade of nails, and stencil letters which take on the coarse, cross-cut texture of the wood. These are but a few of the examples reproduced here.

Unlike stencilled folk art, which finds beauty of a kind by means of placement and repetition, the contemporary artist appears to begin his stencil techniques at these former points of limitation and works in every conceivable and inconceivable direction. The stencil may provide rigid borders or perimeters with respect to form and space, but technique, method, and form of application are curtailed only by the extent of individual creativity.

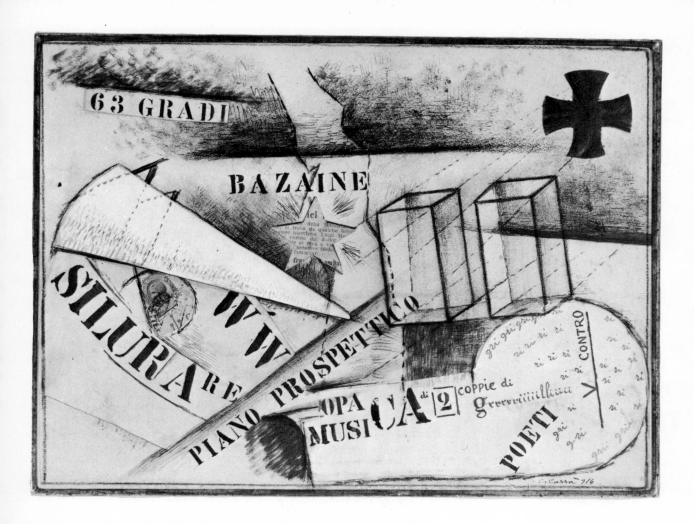

Joffre's Angle of Penetration on the Marne Against Two German Cubes. Multimedia collage by Carlo Carrà (1914). A combination of various inks and charcoal coupled with found elements such as a postage stamp, newsprint, and a thumb print are the principal elements of this composition. Stencil lettering has been added from other sources and also traced directly onto the drawing. The way in which the words are drawn and the nature of the symbols shroud the meaning of the work in mystery. (Reproduced courtesy The Lydia and Harry Lewis Winston Collection: Mrs. Barnett Malbin, Birmingham, Michigan.)

Above. Massacre of the Innocents by Max Ernst (1930). Ernst is a genius at inventing graphic imagery, and in this composition a number of techniques and elements are used to produce an almost surrealistic effect. The stencil form of the man is positioned with much imagination; at one point he seems to be falling away from the painting, at another he is running almost against himself, and at still another he is about to be consumed by a menacing winged monster. (Collection: Simone Collinet.)

Below. Composition RUV. Pen drawing by Fernand Léger (1920). (Reproduced courtesy Kupferstichkabinett, Basel.)

39

The Knife Thrower. Color stencil by Henri Matisse (1947), illustration for the book *Jazz.* Matisse was a master at shaping free form by means of the scissors and worked in cut and pasted gouache for the last four years of his life. Much of his experimentation in this medium employed stencil-like techniques and characteristics insofar as determining and repeating shape and form are concerned. (Reproduced courtesy of the Philadelphia Museum of Art. Photo by A. J. Wyatt.)

The Archer. Sealskin stencil by Niviaksiak of the West Baffin Eskimo Cooperative (1960). Eskimo artists have produced a number of multicolored stencilled compositions, adding to their accomplishments in sculpture and stone printing. (Reproduced courtesy of the National Film Board, Ottawa.)

Collage No. 2 with Wig.
Richard Lindner (1962).
The head in this
composition is very strong
and appears to be both
inside and outside of the
study at the same time.
The number 2 is almost
magical in appearance,
and there is both a
balance and a similarity
between the stencilled
figure and the head.
(Reproduced courtesy of
Mr. and Mrs. Arne H.
Ekstrom, New York.)

Opposite Page

*Parts of the Face—
French Vocabulary
Lesson.* Oil on canvas by
Larry Rivers (1961). The
head has been painted
loosely and is somewhat
incomplete, while the
stencilled words leading
to the parts of the face
are deliberate and
positioned in a most
accurate manner. Compare
the difference between
this very direct form of
stencilling with the
almost poetic use of the
numeral 2 in the Lindner
composition. (Reproduced
courtesy Tate Gallery,
London.)

CHEVEUX

FRONT

SOURCIL

CIL

OEIL

NEZ

JOUE

DENT

LÈVRE

MENTON

43

Opals. Mural by Victor
Vasarely for a university
building in Eisen,
Germany. The artist has
been able to give the
simple shape of the circle
a seemingly limitless
number of variations. By
varying the size of the
circle and by positioning
smaller circles over the
larger ones, diamond-like
figures seem to emerge
mysteriously from the
mural, projecting the
curiosity of seeing round
pegs in a series of square
holes.

Surface 210. Oil on canvas by Giuseppe Capogrossi. A number of similar or related shapes is used to create a composition; though the shapes vary in size, their organization and positioning tend to produce a continuous, single visual effect. (Reproduced courtesy of the Solomon R. Guggenheim Museum, New York.)

Opposite Page

Above. Twenty-Eight Daily Notes.
Construction by Greg Curnoe painted
one each day for 28 consecutive days.
(Reproduced courtesy The Isaacs
Gallery, Toronto.)

Below. View of Victoria Hospital. First
series 1 to 6, marking ink on Latex on
canvas. (Reproduced courtesy Isaacs
Gallery, Toronto, photo by Ayriss.)

These two interesting examples
demonstrate some of the dynamic
potentialities of lettering as a visual
composition. By varying the size of the
letters, small objects or entire walls can
become the canvas. In *View of Victoria
Hospital* some of the letters have been
partially colored, others have been
completely filled in; each letter emerges
with its own color and personality. This
is an economical method of giving the
overall mural a sense of color dynamics.

The D's Testament. Painted and
stencilled construction of wood, steel,
plumbing fixtures, and bicycle parts by
Harry Bouras (1961). Bouras uses
lettering together with three-dimensional
elements and found objects piled upon
each other to produce an effective
composition. There is a visual
relationship between the method by
which the letters are applied and the
way in which the metal construction is
assembled; it is almost as if words and
objects have merged. (Collection, Mr.
and Mrs. James Alter, Chicago.)

Black and White (Walking Woman).
Enamels on canvas by Michael Snow.
(Reproduced courtesy Arts-canada,
Toronto. Photo by Michael Katz.)

Above. A Falling Walking Woman.
Michael Snow.

Below: *Venus Simultaneous*. Mixed
media by Michael Snow. (Reproduced
courtesy The Isaacs Gallery, Toronto.
Photo by John Reeves.)

The artist uses the same figure almost
in the manner in which a poet uses
words. The variation of placement and
positioning creates an entirely new
composition and a new visual
environment in each instance. Snow
employs the profile of the female figure
in a seemingly limitless number of
poses: sideways, backwards, forwards,
upside down, in a repeated series, cut
in half—to explore successfully problems
concerned with two-dimensional space.

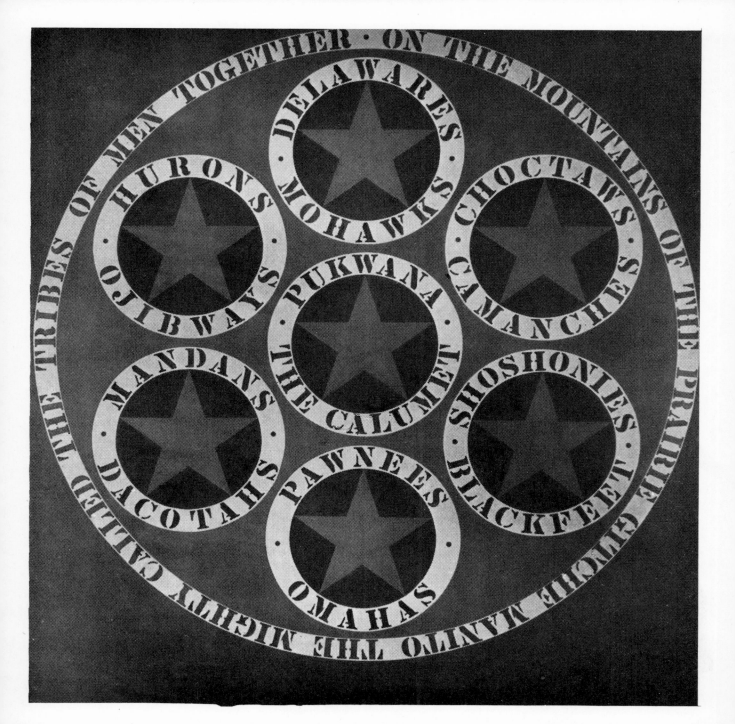

The Calumet. Oil on canvas by Robert Indiana (1961). The artist has created a series of circles and stars of varying sizes and added stencilled letters to unite them as a composition. The words are as clear as labels and extremely legible so that a verbal-visual image is immediately apparent. This kind of stencil lettering is almost the only type face that can be used to convey the information projected through a composition of this quality. (Reproduced courtesy Brandeis University. Photo by John D. Schiff.)

Co-Existence. Combine painting by Robert Rauschenberg (1961). Compared with the Robert Indiana painting in which the words are extremely important, in this composition they are accidental and on found objects. No attempt has been made to make them readable; apparently they do not have to communicate anything. The omitted or obscured letters form quite a contrast to the accuracy of the tribe names projected in *The Calumet.*

51

Above. Detail from *Ten Numbers.* Pencil on paper by Jasper Johns (1960). (Collection of Ted Carey. Reproduced courtesy of Leo Castelli Gallery, New York. Photo by Rudolph Buckhardt.)

Below. Don't Fall and Me. Oil and collage on canvas mounted on wood by Larry Rivers (1966). (Reproduced courtesy of John H. Moore and the Marlborough-Gerson Gallery, Inc., New York. Photo by Nathan Rabin.)

Opposite page, above. Map. Oil painting by Jasper Johns (1963). (Private collection. Reproduced with kind permission of the owner.)

In his drawing, the artist has given each stencilled figure character and personality by his treatment of the background when shading the individual figures. In some instances, though the stencil effect has been almost obliterated by the pencil, it nevertheless remains legible. There is an interplay between the static quality of the stencil and the free application of the pencil strokes. In the map of America, the stencilled letters serve as an identifying force and unify the composition. Johns has succeeded admirably in taking simply patterned and well-remembered objects and images and activating a new awareness of these on the part of the viewer.

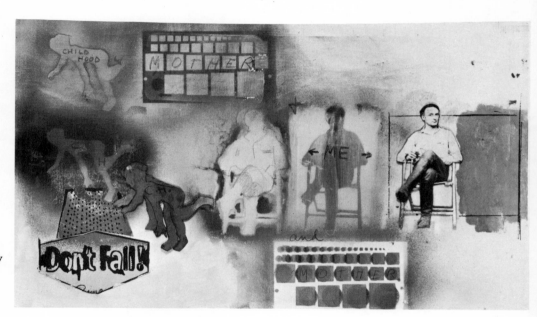

Below. First New York Film Festival Billboard. Oil on canvas by Larry Rivers (1963). (Reproduced courtesy of the Joseph H. Hirshhorn Foundation.)

In *Don't Fall and Me* the artist has made his own stencil figure and treated it in different ways on the canvas. In one instance he is very conscious of the linear form; in another he has produced an almost ghostlike effect by filling the outline in a flat tone and eliminating contrasts. The actual stencil has been pasted right into the composition to form still another figure. In *First New York Film Festival Billboard* the painting is almost an abstract, while the stencilling holds the work together as a composition and, at the same time, communicates its message. There is a playfulness in the way the stencilled letters have been applied: some are filled in, some are left empty, and others have been started with a stencil, then completed by hand-drawing. Though this is a huge billboard, as a composition it has a flexible and free quality.

Campbell's. Silkscreen on wood by Andy Warhol (1964).

Warhol is a master at taking everyday objects and rendering them in an identical form which somehow culminates as a work of art. We are so familiar with these images that they no longer communicate with us. Warhol isolates images from their natural surroundings (e.g., the supermarket shelf) and places them in a new context, such as the art gallery, the poster or the printed page. Looking at them in this new format, we see them as if for the first time. The stencil or screen in this instance could be photographically produced. (Reproduced courtesy of Leo Castelli Gallery, New York. Photo by Rudolph Burckhardt.)

Opposite Page

Jackie. Acrylic and enamel silk-screened on canvas by Andy Warhol (1964).

Instead of isolating one object, the artist has taken a silk-screen stencil and printed it in a series of multiples. The sheer repetition of the same image gives the composition strength and a sense of drama. The background of each image varies in color; this is an economical way of providing tone, mood, and emphasis to a multiple image of this category. (From the Stroher Collection. Reproduced courtesy Ace—Canada—Ltd., Vancouver. Photo by Rudolph Burckhardt.)

Pages 56 and 57

Detail from *Baseball.* Silk-screen ink and oil on canvas by Andy Warhol (1962).

Again the photographic stencil or screen is used in multiple fashion, but this time the image is not clearly delineated. There is a continuous merging of images; everything floats together, and the viewer is conscious of a feeling of movement rather than subject repetition. (Reproduced courtesy of the William Rockhill Nelson Gallery of Art, Atkins Museum of Fine Arts, Kansas City, Missouri. Gift of the Guild of the Friends of Art and a group of the Friends of the Gallery.)

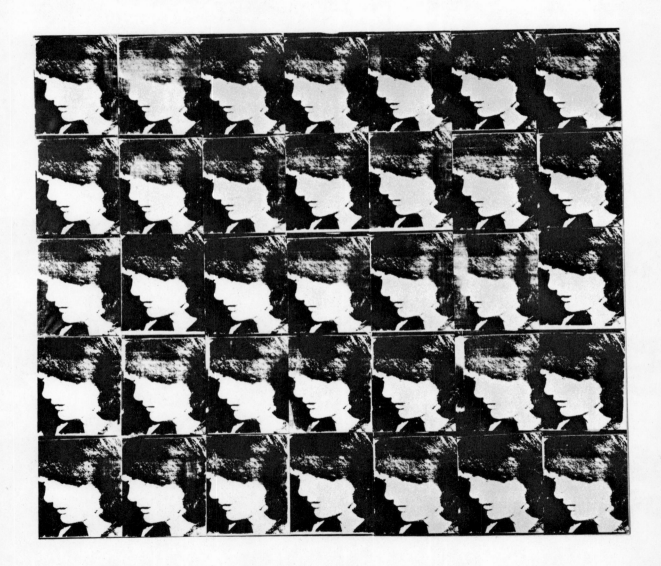

Rhythmic line drawing made with a Spirograph stencil.

4.
Stencil Projects and Art by Norman Laliberté

An almost limitless number of projects can be done by the stencil process. This chapter outlines some of them and concludes with Norman Laliberté's stencil compositions, which often have resulted not from preconceived intention but rather from experimentation while in the process of execution. It is this spirit of exploration on the part of the artist that is paramount to the success of these projects and to the use of the stencil in a serious composition.

Several stencil techniques are demonstrated through the following projects which have been devised by Laliberté, including multiple image, overlapping, off-register, reversing, flopping, printing from the back or reverse side of the stencil after it has been used initially, overprinting, positive and negative forms, using the stencil itself within the composition, stencilling from assembled strips and pieces of paper, creating your own stencil, printing a fragmented stencil, broadening the design of the conventional or ordinary alphabet stencil.

In all of these, and in the Laliberté compositions that follow, the feeling of experimentation as an ingredient vital to the stencilling technique is apparent. Imagination and a simple stencilled letter form can be a wonderful combination, for the solitary letter can be distorted, repeated or overlapped to form a distinctive design, or given an entire personality of its own. The artist is far from bound by the strong and precise form and cut of the stencil; on the contrary, it is at this point where individuality is sparked.

Though the stencil concept or process is traditional, its contemporary technique of application is far from tradition-bound. Laliberté's studies begin with this premise and journey in a number of directions through the use and development of a variety of techniques. Fully conscious of the stencil's potentialities, he creates his own stencil images, prints them, then distorts and distresses them in search of interesting results. He explores with ordinary household objects such as a cookie cutter or a miniature license plate, and through a technique of overlapped impressions we see these familiar forms in a new context. He stencils on top of stencils, monoprints from a stencil, creates intricate stencils with segments of paper doilies, experiments with space and form relationships through stencil repetition. There seem to be no hard or fast rules, only the evolution of processes as the work develops.

The stencil compositions illustrated are a long way from the soft flow of Japanese stencil designs and the precise and organized stencil traditions of the Victorian age. But though different in form, what they have in common is that they are somehow expressive of the time in which they were created. In a highly technical age, the emphasis cannot help but be on originality of technique, and the results that evolve are stimulating, exciting, and extremely free.

Wrapper for a player-piano music roll recorded by Ignace Jan Paderewski. The player piano was one of the first devices to link the stencil concept to automatic mechanical performance. By perforating the roll at different stages, a pattern was created; when processed (or interpreted) by a related mechanical device, it served to activate the piano keys in the desired sequence.

Opposite Page

Today, phototypesetting for printing is created in much the same manner as the music roll. Teletypesetter tape is perforated, then interpreted by a reading device attached to a slugcasting machine which produces the required line of type. The project on the opposite page calls for the use of teletypesetter tapes to create a study or picture. The tape is used as a stencil (that is, paint is pushed through the openings to print a pattern of holes). In this instance, tapes already employed as stencils have been pasted alongside the patterns they produced to form an interesting composition.

I. J. PADEREWSKI

This Music Roll is my interpretation. It was recorded by me for the Duo-Art and I hereby authorize its use with that instrument.

6670-0
Rhapsodie Hongroise
No. 2
PLAYED BY IGNACE JAN PADEREWSKI
Liszt
Made in U. S. A.

D U O – A R T
The AEOLIAN COMPANY

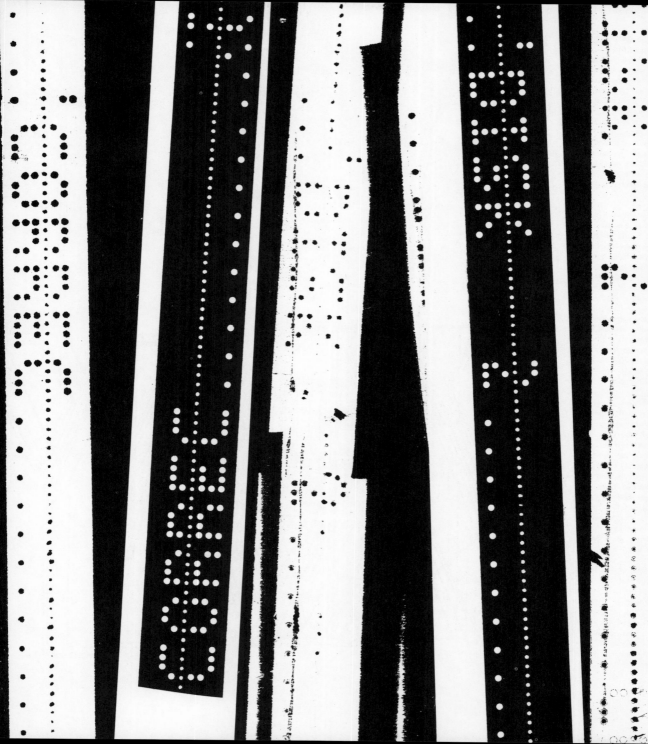

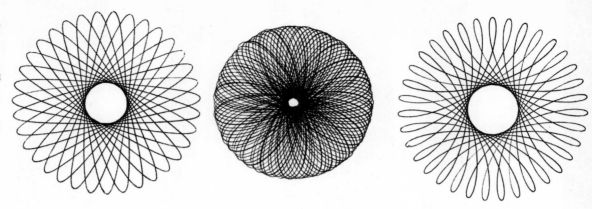

Above. A series of Spirograph drawings. The Spirograph is a form of plastic stencil which, in a way, is a continuation of the player-piano principle (which produced sound) and the teletypesetter concept (which results in manufacturing print). By varying the holes used in the Spirograph, designs of an elegant and lyrical quality can be drawn.

Below. XRAY. In this project, which calls for the use of a conventional stencil, the thickness of the pen lines has been varied, and the letters themselves have been overlapped to produce a word of an almost photonegative quality. The idea is to produce a stencilled word that somehow, through the way in which it is drawn, conveys a feeling of what it represents.

Opposite Page

The letter M. Two different stencil faces— one contemporary (above), the other old-fashioned (below)— were used for these drawings. The project consists of experimenting with the principle of overlapping to produce different effects. In this instance, one style of letter when overlapped produces a very stiff and formal-looking composition, while the other results in a loose, quite natural drawing. What is apparent is that the form of the letter dictates the quality of the stencilled drawing which emerges from experimentation with overlapping.

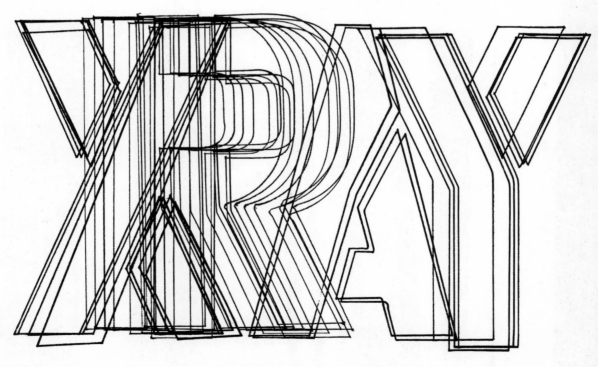

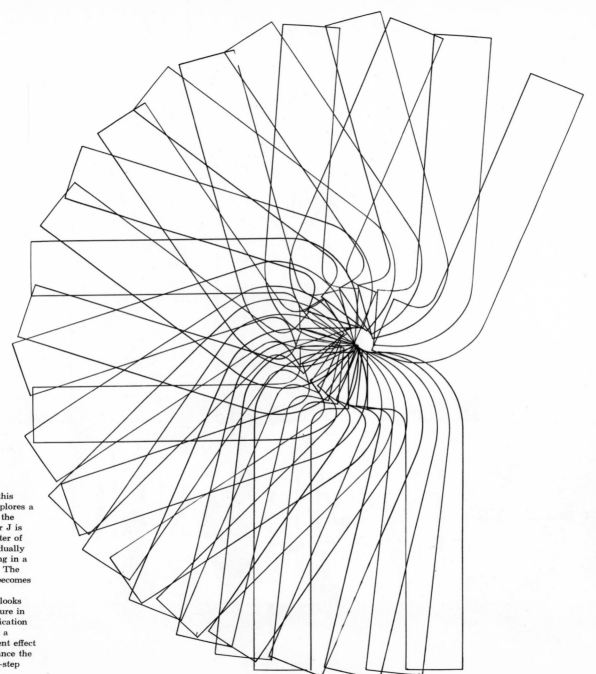

The letter J. In this
project, which explores a
figure in motion, the
curve of the letter J is
placed in the center of
the page and gradually
rotated by drawing in a
fanlike sequence. The
completed form becomes
somewhat three-
dimensional and looks
like a wire sculpture in
shape. Each application
of the J produces a
completely different effect
and tends to advance the
feeling of step-by-step
movement.

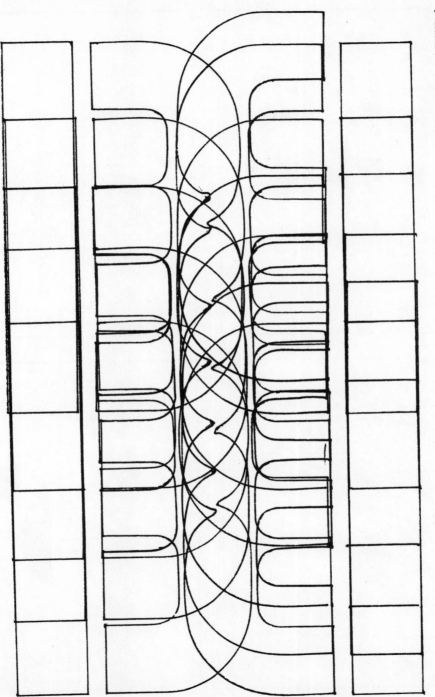

The letter B. In this project, the stencil letter B is moved downward by a series of overlapped tracings; it is then flopped (or reversed) and moved upwards or back toward its starting level. An interesting form is produced by overlapping, the switch in positioning, and the change in the direction of movement.

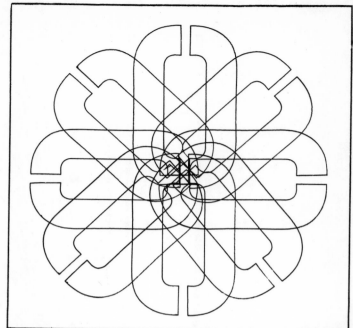

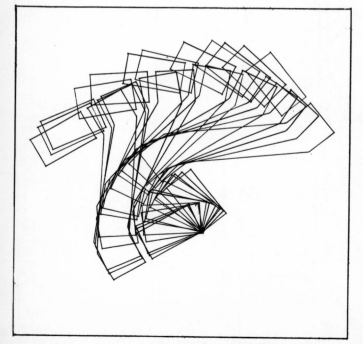

A series of designs created by using only one stencil letter in each composition. In this project the positioning of the letters and the way in which they are moved (reversed, flopped or slightly varied in placement) create new patterns and unusual visual symbols and images.

Instead of using one letter to create a new shape, the actual stencil itself is called upon to produce a different effect. In the project at the top of the page, a printer's roller was used to ink the entire stencil. The inked stencil was then pressed down against a piece of paper. The thickness of the stencil itself formed the small white outline around the letters. In the project at the bottom of the page, the same stencil is used, but here the printer's ink has been diluted to create a gray wash effect.

Pages 68 and 69

This project calls for the use of stencils varying in size and style. In some cases the entire alphabet was printed with an inked roller; in other instances individual stencil letters or figures were placed on top and again printed with a roller. No words or thoughts are being communicated, but the juxtaposition of sizes and different typeface styles illustrates the limitless potential of the stencil's graphic qualities.

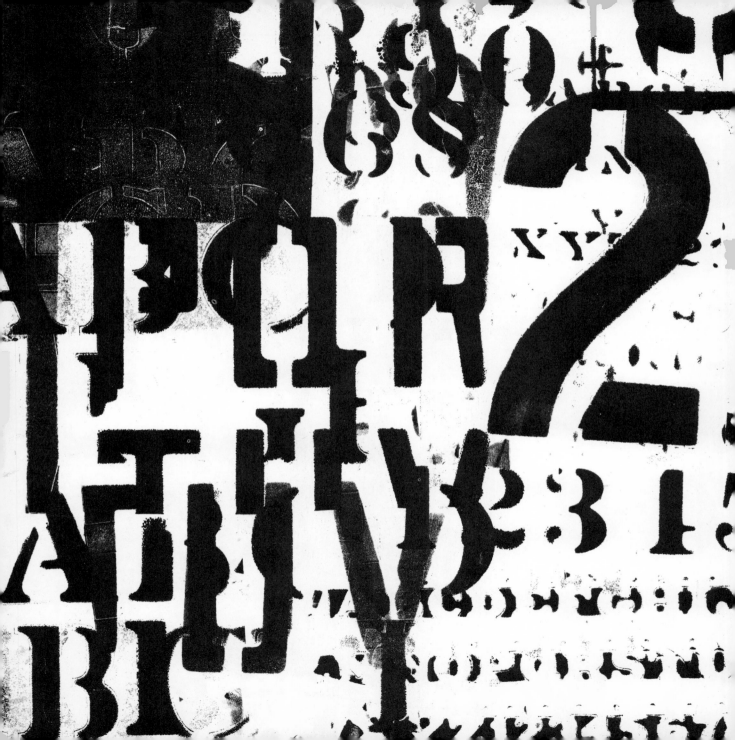

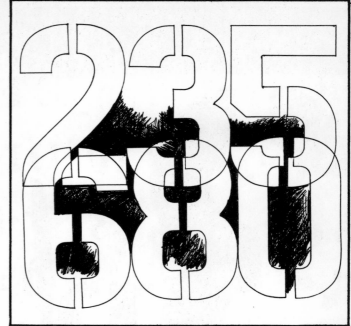

Above left. Individual stencil numbers from 1 to 9 are horizontally delineated in a compressed area.

Above, right. Six figures are traced in a straightforward manner. Some of the background has been inked to give the numerals both a solid and free effect.

Below. The same numbers are traced in two overlapping rows to create both a simple and a complex pattern at the same time. Projects like this explore the relationship between images and space.

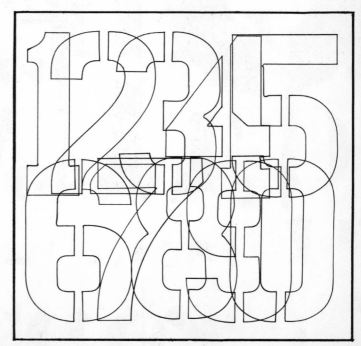

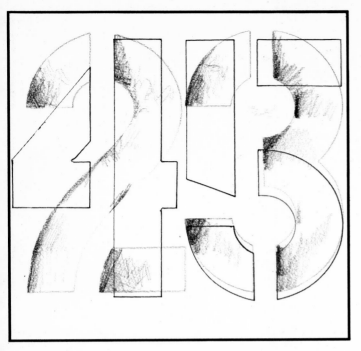

The number 23; one half of the number was treated in a solid manner, the other in an opposite technique to produce an interesting overall effect. Projects such as these illustrate the countless ways in which the stencil can be employed to create exciting and stimulating compositions.

Above, left. Two numbers have been stencilled with a pen to be overlapped by two other numbers of the same size, traced with a charcoal pencil. The contrast between the free pen line and the shadowy line produced by the charcoal is most effective.

Above, right. Again individual figures are used, but this time the stencil was held above the paper to allow the sunlight to filter through the openings. The shadow of the figures reflected on the paper was traced to produce interesting distortions. By changing the angle at which the light comes through the stencil, a great many distorted variations are possible.

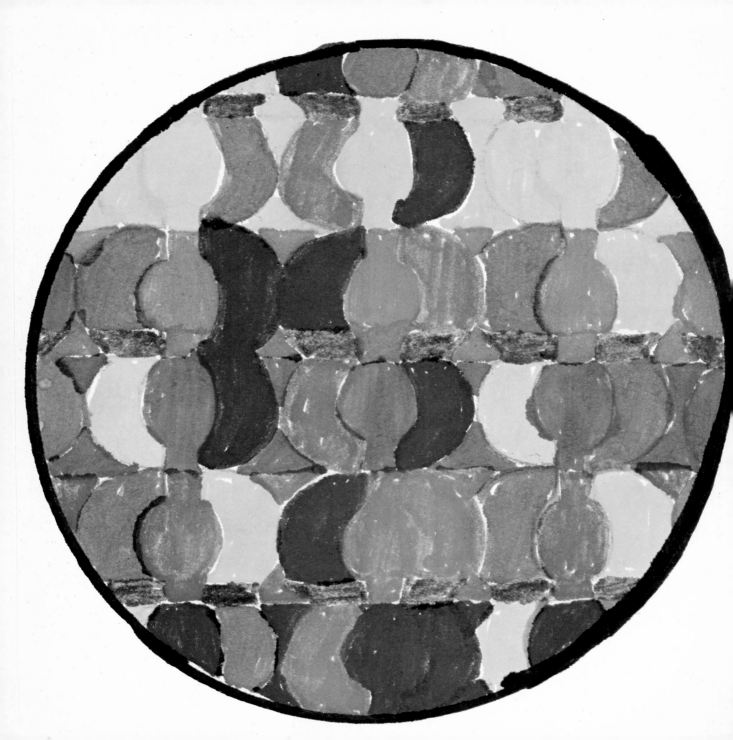

No. 8 by Susan Moschella. Felt pens provide the color; each number has been fragmented, as a number of colors is used to complete individual figures.

Above. The figures 1 to 9 are stencilled one on top of the other to produce an almost frenetic composition.

Below. The figure 8 is isolated and given dimension by enhancing areas both inside and outside of the figure. Experiments such as these explore relationships between space and the anatomy of a graphic figure.

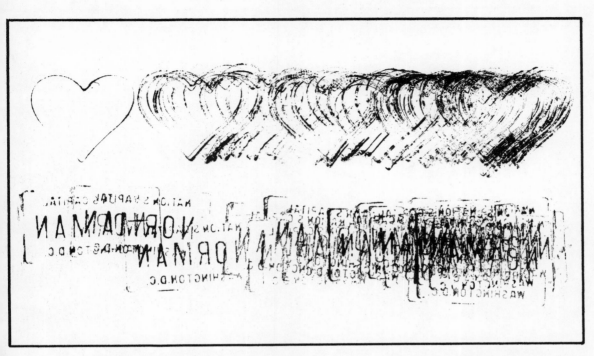

Opposite Page

Composition. Two different sizes of stencil letter were overlapped. Portions of the letters were thickened by adding a freehand ink line over the stencilled line.

Above. A cookie mold in the shape of a heart and a miniature license plate were inked and stamped to illustrate how everyday found objects can be used to create a stencil composition.

Below. A series of overlapping numbers done in a manner almost identical to the way in which the heart example (above) was overprinted.

Pages 76 and 77

Stencil Hieroglyphics. Ink was applied by means of a printer's roller over an entire alphabet stencil cut-out. The ink was allowed to flow through the openings. The inked stencil was then reversed and flopped against the paper; the roller was applied across the back of the stencil, creating the effect of gray and black and reversed letters which have their own characteristics. This process was repeated twelve to fifteen times on the same piece of paper to create a stroboscopic effect. The original work was done on paper five feet wide; because the entire stencil is used, a composition like this should be worked in large dimensions.

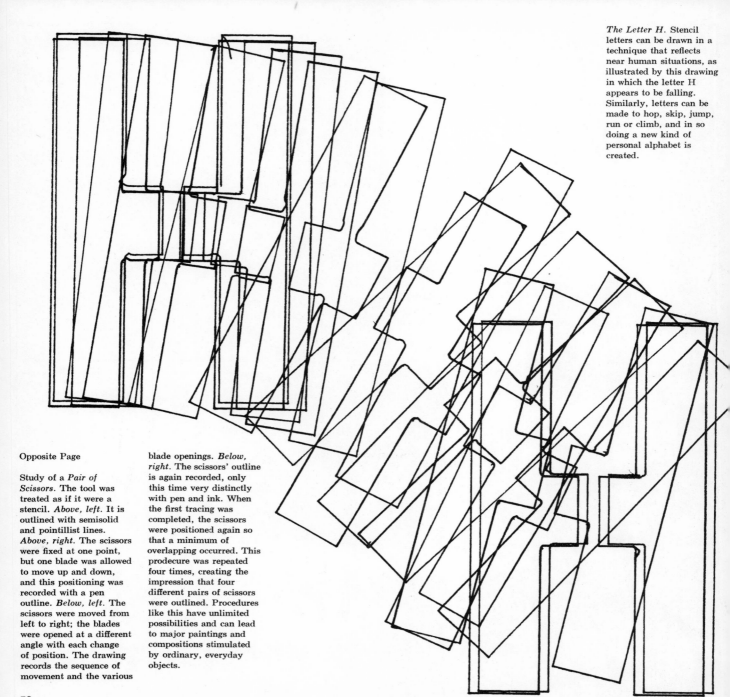

The Letter H. Stencil letters can be drawn in a technique that reflects near human situations, as illustrated by this drawing in which the letter H appears to be falling. Similarly, letters can be made to hop, skip, jump, run or climb, and in so doing a new kind of personal alphabet is created.

Opposite Page

Study of a *Pair of Scissors.* The tool was treated as if it were a stencil. *Above, left.* It is outlined with semisolid and pointillist lines. *Above, right.* The scissors were fixed at one point, but one blade was allowed to move up and down, and this positioning was recorded with a pen outline. *Below, left.* The scissors were moved from left to right; the blades were opened at a different angle with each change of position. The drawing records the sequence of movement and the various blade openings. *Below, right.* The scissors' outline is again recorded, only this time very distinctly with pen and ink. When the first tracing was completed, the scissors were positioned again so that a minimum of overlapping occurred. This prodecure was repeated four times, creating the impression that four different pairs of scissors were outlined. Procedures like this have unlimited possibilities and can lead to major paintings and compositions stimulated by ordinary, everyday objects.

Study of the *Linear Heart*. A piece of cardboard is cut in the shape of a heart which is traced on paper a number of times with lines of varying thickness. A number of different line techniques was used to fill in individual hearts, so they were gradated from light to dark. The variation in line treatment gives each heart a quality of its own. Greater dramatic results can be achieved by tracing more complex items, such as a bicycle.

The same cardboard heart is traced onto paper a number of times, but in this instance the fill-in technique employs varying linear qualities and emphasizes experimentation by producing textures.

Above. The hand is one of the first objects a student traces. It can be treated as a form of stencil, and, as with the scissors, varying effects can be produced by altering palm and finger positions.

Below. Pieces of a jigsaw puzzle also can be traced like a stencil to create interesting designs and drawn structures. In fact, any flat object can become a form of stencil when used in this manner.

Opposite Page

25th Anniversary. Stencils of designs like this or similar die-cut, cardboard decorative objects can be found in variety, stationery, and hardware stores. In this case, the 25th anniversary insignia was placed on a piece of paper, but instead of tracing it in the usual way, the pen delineated its shape by a series of short parallel strokes around its outline. This different treatment is an effective departure from the flowing quality of the usual traced line.

Pages 84 and 85

The same object as in the drawing on page 83 was used as a regular stencil. Ink was pushed through the stencil openings with a printer's roller to produce a regular stencil print. The inked stencil was then flopped onto the paper, and ink was rolled across the back of it, producing a reversed image. The *offset* of the roller (that is, the outline of the stencil that was impressed onto the roller itself) was transferred to the paper. By varying these techniques, an interesting composition was created.

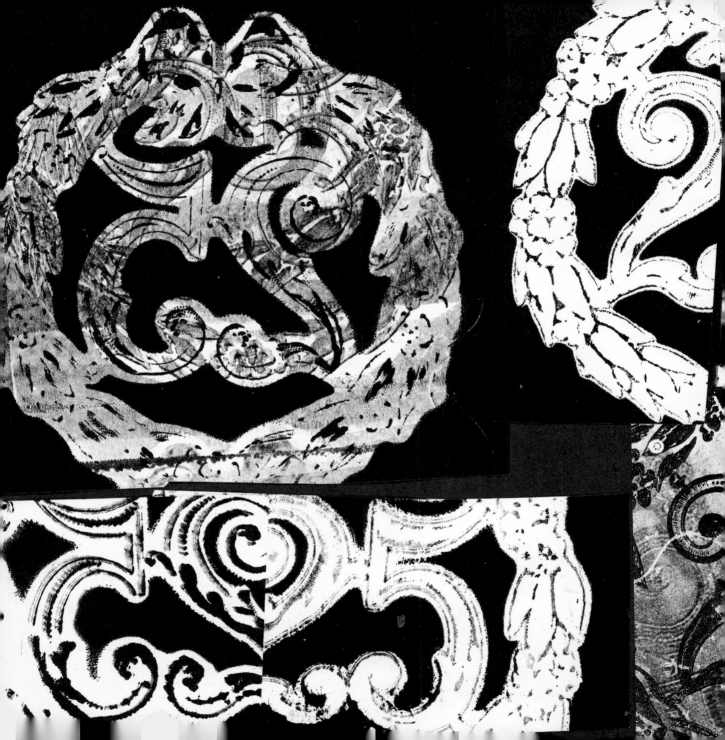

Above. An ordinary paper doily is inked and mounted to form a design. This can be done effectively with lace and macramé, as well.

Below. The Doily Madonna. Segments from paper doilies were arranged to create a composition of figures. In effect, this represents a stencil from which you can print a design impression using charcoal, grease crayon, India ink, paint or printer's ink. Line drawings in any media can be added over the finished work to provide additional detail for embellishment. (Reproduced by kind permission of the National Catholic Reporter.)

Opposite Page

Clown Figure. Segments from a paper doily and felt pens have produced a face which can be stencilled by painting or spraying the openings.

Pages 88 and 89

The First Eve. Instead of using paper doilies, strips and shapes cut from black paper are assembled to form a composition. The composition can be worked as a stencil. The individual strips and shapes can be traced and outlined, or the entire surface of the composition can be rolled with printer's ink. After the strips and shapes were removed, a stencil impression of the composition came into being.

Opposite Page

Shapes and cut-outs of varying sizes are placed on a piece of paper. Printer's ink is rolled over the entire surface with a brayer. The shapes are removed, leaving their stencilled impressions on the paper.

Stencil cut-outs by Jacques Laliberté. Squares of paper are folded over and over again many times, and a pattern is cut into the last fold. When the paper is unfolded, a beautiful design emerges, sometimes complex or geometric, at other times very simple in concept, depending on the intricacies of the pattern cut into the folded segment. Like the paper doily, the design can be used to produce stencilled impressions on paper, fabrics, walls or on textured, angular or circular surfaces.

Pages 92 and 93

The lower right cut-out doily from page 91 was put on paper; the surface was inked with a roller, and then the stencil was lifted, leaving a white negative impression of its design on the paper. The stencil and individual elements of the stencil were reprinted in this manner on the same paper a number of times with the design overlapping at random. Regular stencil numbers were traced into the open spaces.

The top right cut-out doily from page 91 was placed on a paper, and ink was rolled through its openings. The wet stencil was then reversed and flopped (slightly off register) over the design that it had just produced. It was printed again, creating grays, variations of black and an overall image of great photographic quality.

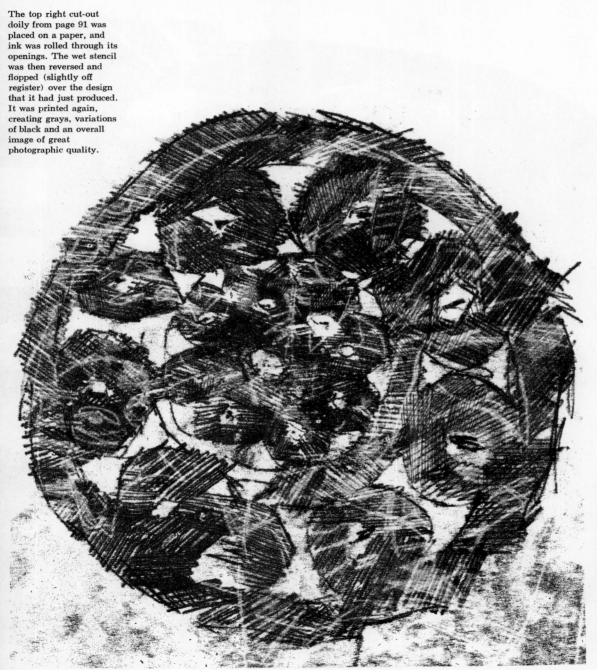

The top left cut-out doily from page 91 was used to create a monoprint. This is done by inking a plate and placing a white paper over its surface. The cut-out stencil is then placed on top of the paper and rubbed with an ordinary pencil. The other side of the white paper picks up the ink from the plate in those areas that are rubbed, and in this way a monoprint of the stencil is formed.

A stencil of a fish is cut from a piece of heavy paper. The fish is inked and then placed against a clean white sheet of paper on which its form is repeated or stencilled.

Pages 98 and 99

A monoprint of the same fish. There is a great deal of difference between the formal solid quality of the stencil and the very soft and free tones of the monoprint impression. To produce the monoprint, a piece of paper was placed against an inked plate. The fish stencil was placed on top of the paper, and the outline and openings of the stencil were drawn or traced, while certain other areas were rubbed by hand. The ink picks up only on those areas touched by the pencil or hand, and in this way a monoprint is produced. The black outline or background border all around the fish was rubbed in (after the monoprint was pulled) with a solid ink roller.

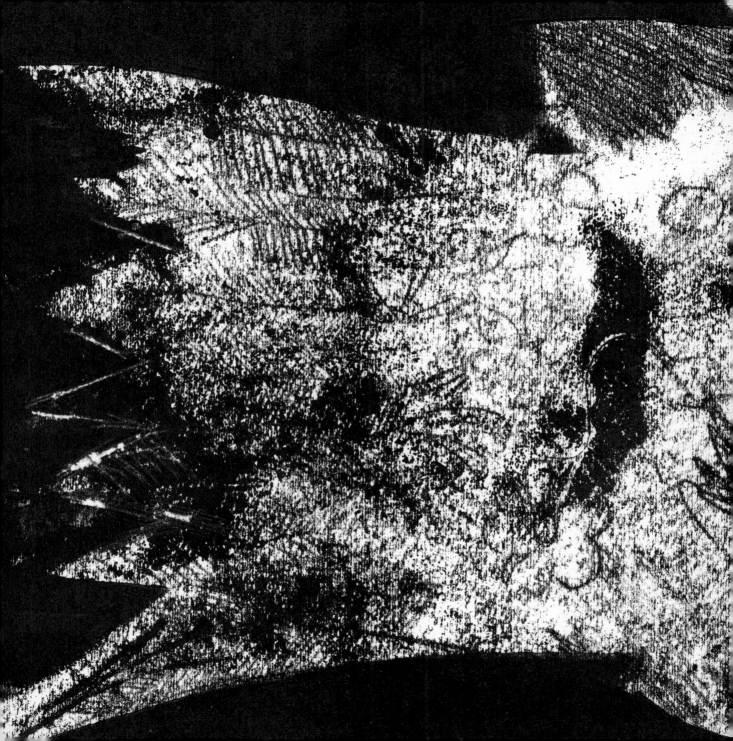

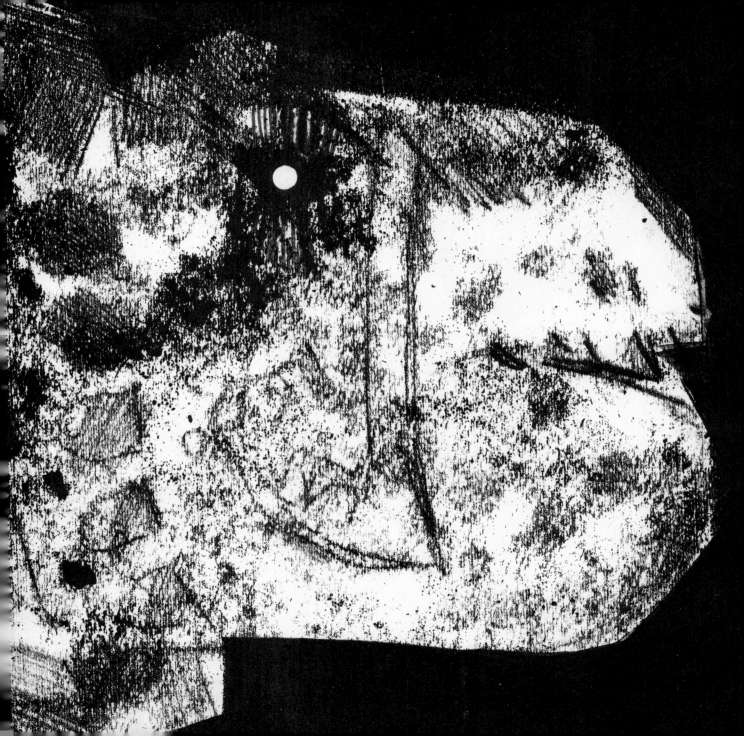

Opposite Page

The Dove. Stencil cut-out in the shape of a bird.

Above

The cut-out dove on the opposite page is used as a stencil in a number of different positions and in various degrees of thinking. A number of stencil techniques are used, including negative and positive versions of the bird, overlapping, reversing or flopping, and off-register printing. This is a good illustration of how one stencilled object can be repeated and used in many directions and moods.

Page 102

The dove stencil on page 100 is repeated four times in four different directions: from right to left, from top to bottom.

Page 103

The same bird has been torn or fragmented, and the pieces are used as a stencil. Pen-and-ink lines were added on the completed work to provide details on the wings, feathers, and eyes.